The Gospel Of Mary Magdalene

By Joseph Lumpkin

Joseph B. Lumpkin

The Gospel of Mary Magdalene

For information about first time authors, contact Fifth Estate, Post Office Box 116, Blountsville, AL 35031.

First Edition

Printed on acid-free paper

Library of Congress Control No: **2006905140**

ISBN: 1933580240

Fifth Estate, 2006

Joseph B. Lumpkin

A Brief Lesson in Theology

The Gospel Of Mary Magdalene is considered a Gnostic Gospel, but what is Gnosticism?

"Gnosticism: A system of religion mixed with Greek and Oriental philosophy of the 1st through 6th centuries A.D. Intermediate between Christianity and paganism, Gnosticism taught that knowledge rather than faith was the greatest good and that through knowledge alone could salvation be attained."

Webster's Dictionary

For centuries the definition of Gnosticism has in itself, been a point of confusion and contention within the religious community. This is due in part, to the ever-broadening application of the term and the fact that various sects of Gnosticism existed as the theology evolved and began to merged into what became mainstream Christianity.

The theology in place at the time of the writing of the Gospel of Mary Magdalene should be considered and understood before attempting to render or read a translation.

To do otherwise would make cloudy and obtuse the translation.

It becomes the duty of both translator and reader to understand the ideas being espoused and the terms conveying those ideas. A grasp of theology, cosmology, and relevant terms is necessary for a clear transmission of the meaning within the text in question.

With this in mind, Gnosticism in the first through third centuries A.D. will be briefly examined.

Like modern Christianity, Gnosticism had various points of view that could be likened to Christian denominations of today. As the theology evolved, Gnosticism began to lose some of its more unorthodox myths. The existence of various sects of Gnosticism, along with the lack of historical documentation, have left scholars in a quandary about exactly what Gnostics believed. Some have suggested that the Gnostics represented a free thinking and idealistic movement much like that of the "Hippie" movement active in the United States during the 1960's. Just as the "Hippie" movement in the U.S. influenced political thought, some early sects of Gnostics began to exert direct influence on the church and its leadership.

Tertullian wrote that between 135 A.D. and 160 A.D. Valentinus, a prominent Gnostic, had great influence in the

Christian church. Valentinus ascended in church hierarchy and became a candidate for the office of bishop of Rome. He lost the election by a narrow margin. Even though Valentinus was outspoken about his Gnostic slant on Christianity, he was a respected member of the Christian community until his death and was probably a practicing bishop in a church of lesser status than the one in Rome.

The main platform of Gnosticism is the ability to transcend the material world through the possession of privileged and directly imparted knowledge. Following this doctrine, Valentinus claimed to have been instructed by a direct disciple of one of Jesus' apostles, a man by the name of Theodas.

Valentinus is considered by many to be the father of modern Gnosticism. His vision of the faith is summarized by G.R.S. Mead in the book "Fragments of a Faith Forgotten."

"The Gnosis in his hands is trying to embrace everything, even the most dogmatic formulation of the traditions of the Master. The great popular movement and its incomprehensibilities were recognized by Valentinus as an integral part of the mighty outpouring; he laboured to weave all together, external and internal, into one piece, devoted his life to the task, and doubtless only at his death perceived that for that age he was attempting the impossible. None but the very few could ever appreciate the ideal of the man, much less understand it. " (Fragments of a Faith Forgotten, p. 297)

Although it appears that there were several sects of Gnosticism, we will attempt to discuss the more universal Gnostic beliefs in the following pages.

The cosmology of Gnosticism is complex and very different from orthodox Christianity. In many ways Gnosticism may appear to be polytheistic or even pantheistic.

The word Gnostic is based on the word "Gnosis," which means "knowledge." The knowledge of the ultimate, unknowable God and man's ability to transcend this material world is how Gnosticism got its name.

To understand some of the basic beliefs of Gnosticism, let us start with common ground between it and modern Christianity. Both believe the world is imperfect, corrupt, and brutal. The blame for this, according to mainstream Christianity, is placed squarely on the shoulders of man himself. With the fall of man, the world was forever changed to the undesirable and harmful place in which we live today.

However, Gnostics reject this view as an incorrect interpretation of the creation myth.

According to Gnostics, the blame is not in ourselves, but in our creator. The creator of this world was himself somewhat less than perfect and in fact, deeply flawed, making mankind the children of a lesser God.

According to the Gnostics, in the beginning a Supreme being called The Father, The Divine All, The Origin, The Supreme God, or The Fullness, emanated the element of existence, both visible and invisible. His intent was not to create but, as light emanates from a flame, so did creation shine forth from God. This manifested the primal element needed for creation. Part of this ethereal material gave form to beings called Aeons. One of these Aeons was called Sophia or Wisdom.

Seeing the Divine flame, Sophia sought to know its origin. She sought to know the very nature of God. Sophia's passion ended in tragedy when she managed to capture a divine and creative spark, which she attempted to duplicate with her own creative force. It was this act that produced the Archons, beings born outside the higher divine realm.

The realm containing the Fullness of the Godhead and Sophia is called the Pleroma or Realm of Fullness. This is the Gnostic heaven. The lesser Gods created in Sophia's failed attempt were cast outside the Pleroma and away from the presence of God. In essence, she threw away and discarded her flawed creations.

She cast it away from her, outside that place [the Pleroma], that no one of the immortal ones [the other Aeons] might see it, for she had created it in ignorance..."

[The Nag Hammadi Library, James M. Robinson, Ed, pp.104 (Harper & Row, 1981, San Franscisco)]

The beings she created were imperfect and oblivious to the Supreme God. Her creations contained deities even less perfect than herself. They are called the powers, the rulers, or the Archons. Their leader is called the Demiurge. These beings would equate to Satan and his demons. It was the flawed, imperfect, spiritually blind Demiurge that became the creator of the material world and all things in it. Thus, man is a child of a lesser, flawed, spiritually blind, and malevolent God.

In Gnostic cosmology the organic or living world is under the control of entities called Aeons, of which Sophia is one. This means the Aeons influence or control intelligence, thought, and mind. Control of the mechanical and inorganic world is given to the Archons. They rule the physical aspects of systems, regulation, limits, and order in the world.

The lesser God that created the world began his existence in a state that was both detached and remote from the Supreme God in aspects both spiritually and physically. The Demiurge, or Half-maker, as he is called, contained only part of the original creative spark of the Supreme Being. He was created with an imperfect nature caused by his distance in lineage and in spirit from the Divine All or Higher God. It is because of his imperfections and limited abilities the lesser God is called the "Half-Maker" or Demiurge.

The Creator God, the Demiurge, and his helpers, the Archons took the stuff of existence produced by the Supreme God and fashioned it into this material world.

Since the Demiurge has no memory of how he came to be alive, he does not realize he was not the true creator. The Demiurge believed he somehow came to create the material world by himself. The Supreme God allowed the Demiurge and Archons to remain deceived.

The Creator God (the Demiurge) intended the material world to be perfect and eternal, but he did not have it in himself to accomplish the feat. What comes forth from a being cannot be greater than the highest part of him, so the world was created flawed and transitory. The Demiurge was imperfect and evil. So was the world he created.

Man was created with a dual nature as the product of the material world of the Demiurge with his imperfect essence, and the spark of God that emanated from the Supreme God through Sophia, which remained in the creator, persisted to form man's spirit.

It is this divine spark in man that calls to its source, the Supreme God, and causes a "divine discontent" that nagging feeling that keeps us questioning if this is all there is. This spark and the feeling it gives us keeps us searching for the truth.

The Creator God seeks to keep man ignorant of his defective state by keeping him enslaved to the material world. By doing so he can continue to receive man's worship and servitude. He does not wish man to recognize or gain knowledge of the true Supreme God. Since he does not know or acknowledge the Supreme God, he views any attempt to worship anything else as spiritual treason.

The opposition of forces set forth in the spiritual battle over the continued enslavement of man and man's spiritual freedom sets up the duality of good and evil in Gnostic theology. The glaring difference between the orthodox Christian viewpoint and the Gnostic viewpoint is that according to Gnostics the creator of the material world is the evil entity and the Supreme God, who was his source, is the good entity. Christians sight John 1:1 saying through Christ, the Word, all things were created.

Only through the realization of man's true state or through death can he escape captivity in the material realm. This means the idea of salvation does not deal with original sin or blood payment. Instead, it focuses on the idea of awakening to the fullness of the truth.

According to Gnostic theology, neither Jesus nor his death can save anyone, but the truth that he came to proclaim can allow a person to save his or her own soul. It is the truth, or realization of the lie of the material world and its God, that sets one on a course of freedom.

To escape the earthly prison and find one's way back to the Pleroma (heaven) and the Supreme God, is the soteriology (salvation doctrine) and eschatology (judgment and reward / heaven doctrine) of Gnosticism.

It may be the idea that personal revelation leads to salvation is what caused the mainline church to declare Gnosticism a heresy. The church can tolerate various theological views better if the views do not undermine the authority of the church to control the people. Gnostic theology placed salvation in the hands of the individual, excluding the need of church and its clergy to grant salvation or absolution.

Gnosticism may be considered polytheistic because it espouses many "levels" of Gods, beginning with an ultimate, unknowable, Supreme God and descending down as he created Sophia and Sophia created the Demiurge (Creator God) each becoming more inferior and limited.

There is a hint of pantheism in Gnostic theology due to the fact that creation occurs because of a deterioration of the Godhead and the dispersion of the creative essence, which eventually devolves into the creation of man.

In the end, there is a universal reconciliation as being after being realizes the existence of the Supreme God and renounces this material world and its inferior creator.

Oddly, the disdain for the material world and its Creator God drives Gnostic theology to far-flung extremes in attitude, beliefs, an actions. Gnostics idolize the serpent in the "Garden of Eden" story. After all, if your salvation hinges on secret knowledge the offer of becoming gods through the knowledge of good and evil sounds wonderful.

Genesis 3 (King James Version)
1Now the serpent was more subtil than any beast of the field which the LORD God had made. And he said unto the woman, Yea, hath God said, Ye shall not eat of every tree of the garden?

2And the woman said unto the serpent, We may eat of the fruit of the trees of the garden:

3But of the fruit of the tree which is in the midst of the garden, God hath said, Ye shall not eat of it, neither shall ye touch it, lest ye die.

4And the serpent said unto the woman, Ye shall not surely die:

5For God doth know that in the day ye eat thereof, then your eyes shall be opened, and ye shall be as Gods, knowing good and evil.

It is because of their vehement struggle against the Creator God and the search for some transcendent truth, that Gnostics held the people of Sodom in high regard. The people of Sodom sought to "corrupt" the messengers sent by their enemy, the Creator God. Anything done to thwart the Demiurge and his minions was considered valiant.

Genesis 19 (King James Version)

1And there came two angels to Sodom at even; and Lot sat in the gate of Sodom: and Lot seeing them rose up to meet them; and he bowed himself with his face toward the ground;

2And he said, Behold now, my lords, turn in, I pray you, into your servant's house, and tarry all night, and wash your feet, and ye shall rise up early, and go on your ways. And they said, Nay; but we will abide in the street all night.

3And he pressed upon them greatly; and they turned in unto him, and entered into his house; and he made them a feast, and did bake unleavened bread, and they did eat.

4But before they lay down, the men of the city, even the men of Sodom, compassed the house round, both old and young, all the people from every quarter:

5And they called unto Lot, and said unto him, Where are the men which came in to thee this night? bring them out unto us, that we may know them.

6And Lot went out at the door unto them, and shut the door after him,

7And said, I pray you, brethren, do not so wickedly.

8Behold now, I have two daughters which have not known man; let me, I pray you, bring them out unto you, and do ye to them as is good in your eyes: only unto these men do nothing; for therefore came they under the shadow of my roof.

9And they said, Stand back. And they said again, This one fellow came in to sojourn, and he will needs be a judge: now will we deal worse with thee, than with them. And they pressed sore upon the man, even Lot, and came near to break the door.

10But the men put forth their hand, and pulled Lot into the house to them, and shut to the door.

To modern Christians, the idea of admiring the serpent, which we believe was Satan, may seem unthinkable. Supporting the idea of attacking and molesting the angels sent to Sodom to warn of the coming destruction seems appalling; but to Gnostics the real evil is the malevolent entity, the Creator God of this world. To destroy his messengers, as was the case in Sodom, would impede his mission. To obtain knowledge of good and evil, as was offered by the serpent in the garden, would set the captives free.

To awaken the inner knowledge of the true God was the battle. The material world was designed to prevent the awakening by entrapping, confusing, and distracting the spirit of man. The aim of Gnosticism was the spiritual awakening and freedom of man.

Gnostics, in the age of the early church, would preach to converts (novices) about this awakening, saying the novice must awaken the God within himself and see the trap that is the material world. Salvation comes from the recognition or knowledge contained in this spiritual awakening.

Not all people are ready or willing to accept the Gnosis. Many are bound to the material world and are satisfied to be only as and where they are. These have mistaken the Creator God for the Supreme God and do not know there is anything beyond the Creator God or the material existence. These people know only the lower or earthly wisdom and not the higher wisdom above the Creator God. They are referred to as "dead."

Those who were truly enlightened believed the world could no longer influence their spiritual journey. The material world cannot impede the spiritual world since the two are in opposition. Such an attitude influenced some Gnostics toward Stoicism and others toward Epicureanism. As human nature is predisposed to do, most took up the more wanton practices, believing that nothing done in their earthly bodies would affect their spiritual lives. Whether it was excesses in sex, alcohol, food, or any other sorted debauchery, the Gnostics were safe within their faith, believing nothing spiritually bad could come of their earthly adventures.

The world was out of balance, inferior, and corrupt. The spirit was perfect and intact. It was up to the Gnostics to tell the story, explain the error, and awaken the world to the light of truth. The Supreme God had provided a vehicle to help in their effort. He had created a teacher of light and truth.

Since the time of Sophia's mistaken creation of the Archons, there was an imbalance in the cosmos. The Supreme God began to re-established the balance by producing Christ to teach and save man. This left only Sophia, now in a fallen and bound state, along with the Demiurge, and the Archons to upset the cosmic equation. In this theology one might loosely equate the Supreme God to the Christian Father God, Demiurge to Satan, the Archons to demons, the Pleroma to heaven, and Sophia to the creative force. According to some Gnostic sects, Sophia represents the Holy Spirit.

For those who seek that which is beyond the material world and its flawed creator, the Supreme God has sent Messengers of Light to awaken the divine spark of the Supreme God within us. This part of us will call to the True God as deep calls to deep. The greatest and most perfect Messenger of Light was the Christ. He is also referred to as The Good, Christ, Messiah, and The Word. He came to reveal the Divine Light to us in the form of knowledge.

According to the Gnostics, Christ came to show us our own divine spark and to awaken us to the illusion of the material world and its flawed maker. He came to show us the way back to the divine Fullness (The Supreme God). The path to enlightenment is the knowledge sleeping within each of us. Christ came to show us the Christ spirit living in each of us. Individual ignorance or the refusal to awaken our internal divine spark is the only original sin. Christ is the only Word spoken by God that can awaken us. Christ is also the embodiment of the Word itself. He is part of the original transmission from the Supreme God that has taken form on the earth to awaken the soul of man so that man may search beyond the material world.

One Gnostic view of the Incarnation was "docetic," which is an early heretical position that Jesus was never actually present in the flesh, but only appeared to be human. He was a spiritual being and his human appearance was only an illusion.

Most Gnostics held that the Christ spirit indwelt the earthly Jesus at the time of his baptism by John, at which time Jesus received the name, and thus the power, of the Lord or Supreme God.

The Christ spirit departed from Jesus' body before his death. These two viewpoints remove the idea of God sacrificing himself as an atonement for the sins of man.

Since there is a distinction in Gnosticism between the man Jesus and the Light of Christ that came to reside within him, it is not contrary to Gnostic beliefs that Mary was the consort and wife of Jesus. Neither would it be blasphemous for them to have children.

According to Gnostic theology, nothing can come from the material world that is not flawed. Because of this viewpoint Gnostics did not believe that Christ could have been a corporeal being. Thus, there must be some separation or distinction between Jesus, as a man, and Christ, as a spiritual being born from the Supreme, unrevealed, and eternal God.

To look closer at this theology, we turn to Valentinus, the driving force of early Gnosticism, for an explanation. Valentinus divides Jesus Christ into two very distinct parts; Jesus, the man, and Christ, the anointed spiritual messenger of God. These two forces met in the moment of Baptism when the Spirit of God came to rest on Jesus and the Christ power entered his body.

Jesus, the man, became a vessel containing the Light of God, called Christ. In the Gnostic view we all could and should become Christs, carrying the Truth and Light of God. We are all potential vehicles of the same Spirit that Jesus held within him when he was awakened to the Truth.

This means that the suffering and death of Jesus takes on much less importance in the Gnostic view, since Jesus was simply part of the corrupt world and was suffering the indignities of this world as any man would. In this viewpoint, he could have been married and been a father without disturbing Gnostic theology in the least.

The Gnostic texts seem to divide man into parts., although at times the divisions are somewhat unclear. The divisions alluded to may include the soul, which is the will of man; the spirit, which is depicted as wind or air (pneuma) and contains the holy spark that is the spirit of God in man; and the material human form, the body. The mind of man sits as a mediator between the soul, or will, and the spirit, which is connected to God.

Without the light of the truth the spirit is held captive by the lesser God (the Demiurge), which enslave man. This entrapment is called "sickness." It is this sickness that the Light came to heal us and set us free. The third part of man, which is his material form, is considered a weight, an anchor, and a hindrance, keeping man attached to the corrupted earthly realm.

As we read the text, we must realize that Gnosticism conflicts with traditional Christianity. Overall theology can rise and fall upon small words and terms. If Jesus was not God, his death and thus his atonement meant nothing. His suffering meant nothing. Even the resurrection meant nothing if one's view of Jesus was that he was not human to begin with, as was true with some Gnostics. Think of the implications to the orthodox Christian world if the spirit of God departed from Jesus as it fled and laughed as the body was crucified. This is the implication of the Gnostic interpretation of the death of Jesus when he cries out, "My power, my power, why have you left me," as the Christ spirit left his body before his death.

What are the ramifications to the modern Christian if the Creator God himself is more evil than his creation?

Although, in time, the creation myth and other Gnostic differences began to be swept under the rug, it was the division between Jesus and the Christ spirit that put them at odds with the emerging orthodox church. At the establishment of the doctrine of the trinity, the mainline church firmly set a divide between themselves and the Gnostics.

To this day there is a battle raging in the Christian world as believers and seekers attempt to reconcile today's Christianity to the sect of the early Christian church called, "Gnosticism."

Gnostic texts often use sex as a metaphor for spiritual union and release. Since the Godhead itself has both a masculine element of the Supreme God, who is the Father, and a feminine element of Sophia, sexual terms are used freely. The sexual metaphor is expanded in the story of the Supreme God giving rise to Sophia as he spewed forth the essence of everything. According to some sects Sophia became the creator or mother of both angels and lesser Gods, including the creator of the material world, the Demiurge.

Sexual duality found in Gnosticism allows for more reverence and acceptance of women in the Gnostic worship. Owing to this, the concept that Mary Magdalene was somehow special to Jesus, as is reported in the *Gospel of Philip*, or that he may have shared spiritual concepts with her that were unknown to the male apostles, as told in the *Gospel of Mary Magdalene*, is not so difficult to comprehend.

The sexual metaphors used in the Gnostic texts have fanned the flames of great controversy and speculation. It has been widely accepted that societal norms of the time dictated that Jewish men were to be married by the age of thirty. This certainly applied to Rabbis, since marriage and procreation were considered divine commands. Since Jesus is referred to by the title of Rabbi in the Bible it has been noted that his marital status would have placed him into a very small minority in the culture at the time. Thus, some Gnostic followers use this observation to bolster the idea Jesus was married. This idea was held by those who thought that Jesus, the man, was the vehicle for the Christ sprit. For those who thought Jesus was an illusion placed on us by Christ while he was on earth the idea of a spirit mingling with flesh was out of the question.

If one were to examine the writings of Solomon, the play on words between the sexual and the spiritual aspects can be seen clearly. The Gnostics simply expanded on the theme.

Song of Solomon 1 (King James Version)

1The song of songs, which is Solomon's.

2Let him kiss me with the kisses of his mouth: for thy love is better than wine.

3Because of the savour of thy good ointments thy name is as ointment poured forth, therefore do the virgins love thee.

4Draw me, we will run after thee: the king hath brought me into his chambers: we will be glad and rejoice in thee, we will remember thy love more than wine:

Song of Solomon 2

16My beloved is mine, and I am his: he feedeth among the lilies.

17Until the day break, and the shadows flee away, turn, my beloved, and be thou like a roe or a young hart upon the mountains of Bether.

Song of Solomon 3

1By night on my bed I sought him whom my soul loveth: I sought him, but I found him not.

2I will rise now, and go about the city in the streets, and in the broad ways I will seek him whom my soul loveth: I sought him, but I found him not…

Song of Solomon 5

1I am come into my garden, my sister, my spouse: I have gathered my myrrh with my spice; I have eaten my honeycomb with my honey; I have drunk my wine with my milk: eat, O friends; drink, yea, drink abundantly, O beloved.

2I sleep, but my heart waketh: it is the voice of my beloved that knocketh, saying, Open to me, my sister, my love, my dove, my undefiled: for my head is filled with dew, and my locks with the drops of the night.

3I have put off my coat; how shall I put it on? I have washed my feet; how shall I defile them?

4My beloved put in his hand by the hole of the door, and my bowels were moved for him.

5I rose up to open to my beloved; and my hands dropped with myrrh, and my fingers with sweet smelling myrrh, upon the handles of the lock.

Song of Solomon 7

1How beautiful are thy feet with shoes, O prince's daughter! the joints of thy thighs are like jewels, the work of the hands of a cunning workman.

2Thy navel is like a round goblet, which wanteth not liquor: thy belly is like an heap of wheat set about with lilies.

3Thy two breasts are like two young roes that are twins.

Sex is a mystical experience and religion is replete with sexual allegories. Proceeding from the two points of sexual metaphor in Gnostic literature and the likelihood of marriage among the population of Jewish men, controversy arose when speculation began as to whether Jesus could have married. The flames of argument roared into inferno proportions when the translation of the books of Philip and Mary Magdalene were published.

And the companion (Consort) was Mary of Magdala (Mary Magdalene). The Lord loved Mary more than all the other disciples and he kissed her often on her mouth (the text is missing here and the word "mouth" is assumed). The others saw his love for Mary and asked him: "Why do you love her more than all of us?" The Savior replied, "Why do I not love you in the same way I love her?" Gospel of Philip

Peter said to Mary; "Sister we know that the Savior loved you more than all other women. Tell us the words of the Savior that you remember and know, but we have not heard and do not know. Mary answered him and said; "I will tell you what He hid from you."
The Gospel of Mary Magdalene

Seizing on the texts above, writers of both fiction and non-fiction allowed their pens to run freely amidst conjecture and speculation of marriage and children between Jesus and Mary Magdalene.

The writers *of The Da Vinci Code and Holy Blood, Holy Grail* took these passages and expanded them into storylines that have held readers captive with anticipation.

Did Jesus take Mary to be his wife? Could the couple have produced children? Gnostic theology leaves open the possibility.

Who Was Mary Magdalene

As was customary in Bible times, the last name of the person was connected to his or her place of ancestry. This is evidenced in the fact that Jesus was called, "Jesus of Nazareth." Mary came from a town called Magdala, which was 120 miles north of Jerusalem on the shores of the Sea of Galilee. Magdala Tarichaea may have been the full name of the town. Magdala means tower, and Tarichaea means salted fish. The little village had the optimistic name of "The Tower of Salted Fish." The main business of the area was fishing and there is a good chance that Mary worked in the fish markets.

The Jewish text, "Lamentations Raba," mentions a town called "Magdala," and says Magdala was judged by God and destroyed because of its fornication. This could explain western Christianity's assumption that Mary Magdalene was the prostitute caught in adultery and presented to Jesus.

In fact, we have linked Mary Magdalene with many of the women in the New Testament who were redeemed or forgiven. This is a powerful and rich myth that resonates with both men and women who have fallen from grace and seek redemption. However, the Bible never says that Mary Magdalene was ever a prostitute.

Luke does not name her as the women who washes the feet of Jesus with her hair.

Luke 7 (King James version)

36And one of the Pharisees desired him that he would eat with him. And he went into the Pharisee's house, and sat down to meat.

37And, behold, a woman in the city, which was a sinner, when she knew that Jesus sat at meat in the Pharisee's house, brought an alabaster box of ointment,

38And stood at his feet behind him weeping, and began to wash his feet with tears, and did wipe them with the hairs of her head, and kissed his feet, and anointed them with the ointment.

39Now when the Pharisee which had bidden him saw it, he spake within himself, saying, This man, if he were a prophet, would have known who and what manner of woman this is that toucheth him: for she is a sinner.

40And Jesus answering said unto him, Simon, I have somewhat to say unto thee. And he saith, Master, say on.

41There was a certain creditor which had two debtors: the one owed five hundred pence, and the other fifty.

42And when they had nothing to pay, he frankly forgave them both. Tell me therefore, which of them will love him most?

43Simon answered and said, I suppose that he, to whom he forgave most. And he said unto him, Thou hast rightly judged.

44And he turned to the woman, and said unto Simon, Seest thou this woman? I entered into thine house, thou gavest me no water for my feet: but she hath washed my feet with tears, and wiped them with the hairs of her head.

45Thou gavest me no kiss: but this woman since the time I came in hath not ceased to kiss my feet.

46My head with oil thou didst not anoint: but this woman hath anointed my feet with ointment.

47Wherefore I say unto thee, Her sins, which are many, are forgiven; for she loved much: but to whom little is forgiven, the same loveth little.

48And he said unto her, Thy sins are forgiven.

49And they that sat at meat with him began to say within themselves, Who is this that forgiveth sins also?

50And he said to the woman, Thy faith hath saved thee; go in peace.

There is never a name given to the woman caught in the act of adultery.

John 8 (King James Version)

1Jesus went unto the mount of Olives.

2And early in the morning he came again into the temple, and all the people came unto him; and he sat down, and taught them.

3And the scribes and Pharisees brought unto him a woman taken in adultery; and when they had set her in the midst,

4They say unto him, Master, this woman was taken in adultery, in the very act.

5Now Moses in the law commanded us, that such should be stoned: but what sayest thou?

6This they said, tempting him, that they might have to accuse him. But Jesus stooped down, and with his finger wrote on the ground, as though he heard them not.

7So when they continued asking him, he lifted up himself, and said unto them, He that is without sin among you, let him first cast a stone at her.

8And again he stooped down, and wrote on the ground.

9And they which heard it, being convicted by their own conscience, went out one by one, beginning at the eldest, even unto the last: and Jesus was left alone, and the woman standing in the midst.

10When Jesus had lifted up himself, and saw none but the woman, he said unto her, Woman, where are those thine accusers? hath no man condemned thee?

11She said, No man, Lord. And Jesus said unto her, Neither do I condemn thee: go, and sin no more.

12Then spake Jesus again unto them, saying, I am the light of the world: he that followeth me shall not walk in darkness, but shall have the light of life.

The only clear history we have is a single statement that it was Mary that was once demon-possessed.

Luke 8 (King James Version)

1And it came to pass afterward, that he went throughout every city and village, preaching and shewing the glad tidings of the kingdom of God: and the twelve were with him,

2And certain women, which had been healed of evil spirits and infirmities, Mary called Magdalene, out of whom went seven devils,

3And Joanna the wife of Chuza Herod's steward, and Susanna, and many others, which ministered unto him of their substance.

Here is what we know with certainty:

She was a woman who followed Jesus as he ministered and preached.

Luke 8:1-3: Afterward, Jesus journeyed from one town and village to another, preaching and proclaiming the good news of the kingdom of God. Accompanying him were the Twelve and some women who had been cured of evil spirits and infirmities, Mary, called Magdalene, from whom seven demons had gone out, Joanna, the wife of Herod's steward Chuza, Susanna, and many others who provided for them out of their resources.

She was there when Jesus was crucified.

Mark 15:40: There were also some women looking on from a distance, among whom were Mary Magdalene, and Mary the mother of James the Less and Joses, and Salome.
Matthew 27:56: Among them was Mary Magdalene, and Mary the mother of James and Joseph, and the mother of the sons of Zebedee.

John 19:25: But standing by the cross of Jesus were His mother, and His mother's sister, Mary the wife of Clopas, and Mary Magdalene.

She continued to believe in Jesus after he was killed.

Mark 15:47: Mary Magdalene and Mary the mother of Joses were looking on to see where He was laid.

Matthew 27:61: And Mary Magdalene was there, and the other Mary, sitting opposite the grave.

Matthew 28:1: Now after the Sabbath, as it began to dawn toward the first day of the week, Mary Magdalene and the other Mary came to look at the grave.

Mark 16:1: When the Sabbath was over, Mary Magdalene, and Mary the mother of James, and Salome, bought spices, so that they might come and anoint Him.

She was the first to realize and announce the resurrection of Jesus.

John 20:1: Now on the first day of the week Mary Magdalene came early to the tomb, while it was still dark, and saw the stone already taken away from the tomb.

Mark 16:9: Now after He had risen early on the first day of the week, He first appeared to Mary Magdalene, from whom He had cast out seven demons.

John 20:18: Mary Magdalene came, announcing to the disciples, "I have seen the Lord," and that He had said these things to her.

Luke 24: But at daybreak on the first day of the week [the women] took the spices they had prepared and went to the tomb. They found the stone rolled away from the tomb; but when they entered, they did not find the body of the Lord Jesus. While they were puzzling over this, behold, two men in dazzling garments appeared to them. They were terrified and bowed their faces to the ground. They said to them, "Why do you seek the living one among the dead?

He is not here, but he has been raised. Remember what he said to you while he was still in Galilee, that the Son of Man must be handed over to sinners and be crucified, and rise on the third day." And they remembered his words.

Then they returned from the tomb and announced all these things to the eleven and to all the others.

The women were Mary Magdalene, Joanna, and Mary the mother of James; the others who accompanied them also told this to the apostles, but their story seemed like nonsense and they did not believe them.

It is the myth woven into the story of Mary that empowers her to us. To many, she is captive, possessed, enslaved, caught in the midst of crime and tragedy, but at once redeemed, set free, and loved by God himself. She is hope and triumph. She represents the power of truth and love to change the life of the lowest and most powerless of us. She is you and me in search of God.

History of The Gospel Of Mary Magdalene

While traveling and researching in Cairo in 1896, German scholar, Dr. Carl Reinhardt, acquired a papyrus containing Coptic texts entitled the Revelation of John, the Wisdom of Jesus Christ, and the Gospel of Mary.

Before setting about to translate his exciting find, two world wars ensued, delaying publication until 1955. By then the Nag Hammadi collection had also been discovered.

Two of the texts in his codex, the Revelation of John, and the Wisdom of Jesus Christ, were included there. Importantly, the codex preserves the most complete surviving copy of the Gospel of Mary, named for its supposed author, Mary of Magdala. Two other fragments of the Gospel of Mary written in Greek were later unearthed in archaeological digs at Oxyrhynchus in Northern Egypt.

In all, to date, two third-century Greek manuscripts and a more intact fifth-century Coptic manuscript have been unearthed.

The Gospel of Mary was probably penned between 120 and 180 A.D. The original languages was Greek.

All of the various fragments were brought together to

form the translation presented here. However, even with all of the fragments assembled, the manuscript of the Gospel of Mary is missing pages 1 to 6 and pages 11 to 14. These pages included sections of the text up to chapter 4, and portions of chapter 5 through chapter 8.

Although the text of the Gospel of Mary is incomplete, the text presented below serves to shake the very concept of our assumptions of early Christianity as well as Christ's possible relationship to Mary of Magdala, whom we call Mary Magdalene.

About the Text

As with any book, it is impossible to please everyone. If one publishes a book with commentary, there will be a portion of the readership that will prefer the translated text only, having determined to make up their minds as to the meaning without the input of the author. If one publishes a simple text, there will be those who will purchase a book hoping to obtain a commentary to help them to better understand the text. In an attempt to serve both sides of the readership, this book contains a translation without commentary as well as a translation with commentary and verses from the Holy Bible that parallel the text. In the section with commentary the text of the Gospel of Mary Magdalene is bold. The Bible quotes are italicized, and the author's words are in plain text.

The Gospel of Mary Magdalene (With Commentary)

(Pages 1 to 6, containing chapters 1 to 3, could not be recovered. The text starts on page 7, chapter 4.)

Chapter 4

21 (And they asked Jesus), "Will matter then be destroyed or not?"

Here, we must assume that a deep and thoughtful discussion was in progress regarding the end of time. In many of the apocalyptic books of the time there were various outcomes. One possibility was the total destruction of the earth. Whether reunited in Heaven, or on a newly created earth, after the time of destruction there is always a time and place the righteous will be gathered together with God. This is reflected in the Second Book of Peter of the Holy Bible.

2 Peter 3 (King James Version)

1This second epistle, beloved, I now write unto you; in both which I stir up your pure minds by way of remembrance:

2That ye may be mindful of the words which were spoken before by the holy prophets, and of the commandment of us the apostles of the Lord and Saviour:

3Knowing this first, that there shall come in the last days scoffers, walking after their own lusts,

4And saying, Where is the promise of his coming? for since the fathers fell asleep, all things continue as they were from the beginning of the creation.

5For this they willingly are ignorant of, that by the word of God the heavens were of old, and the earth standing out of the water and in the water

6Whereby the world that then was, being overflowed with water, perished:

7But the heavens and the earth, which are now, by the same word are kept in store, reserved unto fire against the day of judgment and perdition of unGodly men.

8But, beloved, be not ignorant of this one thing, that one day is with the Lord as a thousand years, and a thousand years as one day.

9The Lord is not slack concerning his promise, as some men count slackness; but is longsuffering to us-ward, not willing that any should perish, but that all should come to repentance.

10But the day of the Lord will come as a thief in the night; in the which the heavens shall pass away with a great noise, and the elements shall melt with fervent heat, the earth also and the works that are therein shall be burned up.

11Seeing then that all these things shall be dissolved, what manner of persons ought ye to be in all holy conversation and Godliness,

12Looking for and hasting unto the coming of the day of God, wherein the heavens being on fire shall be dissolved, and the elements shall melt with fervent heat?

13Nevertheless we, according to his promise, look for new heavens and a new earth, wherein dwelleth righteousness.

14Wherefore, beloved, seeing that ye look for such things, be diligent that ye may be found of him in peace, without spot, and blameless.

22) The Savior said, "All nature, all things formed, and all things created exist in and with one another, and they will be dissolved again into their own elements (origins).

Later, we will read that God is "dissolved " into all things. In this case we assume the dissolving of matter is a disassembling of the basic building blocks of matter. This leads to pantheism in that the perturbation of the essence of the Godhead by Sophia disseminated the divine force into lower realms, resulting in the creation of the material world by use of the misappropriation of the creative force and essence by a lower entity.

23) This is because it is the nature of matter to return to its original elements.

24) If you have an ear to hear, listen to this."

It should be noted that the word "element" is used.

According to Webster's Dictionary, element is defined as:

element |ˈeləmənt| |ˌɛləmənt| |ˌɛlɪm(ə)nt| noun

"A substance that cannot be decomposed by any known method. Each element is distinguished by its atomic number, i.e., the number of protons in the nuclei of its atoms.

Any of the four substances – earth, air, fire, water – formerly believed to constitute all physical matter. Any of these four substances thought of as the natural environment of a class of living beings.

(elements) (in church use) the bread and wine of the Eucharist."

The definition is important because it hints at the power and heat needed to break apart all complex substances and reduce them to their basic building blocks. Striping covalent and ionic bonds, ripping apart molecules, and bringing all matter back to its original atomic principles or elements demands intense energy.

As stated in the above definition, the word, "element" has other underlying meanings regarding the Host or Eucharist as well as the basic nature of human personality.

25) Peter said to him, "Since you have explained all things to us, tell us this also: What sin did the world commit (what sin is in the world)?"

26) The Savior said, "There is no sin (of the world). Each person makes his own sin when he does things like adultery (in the same nature as adultery). This is called sin.

27) That is why the Good (sinless Christ) came to be among you. He came to restore every nature to its basic root."

In Gnosticism, the concept of original sin is rooted in personal ignorance. This is the rejection of the knowledge that will free one from the material world. Adultery is simply a signpost showing that the person is clinging to what the world offers and shunning the truth.

This idea is in direct conflict with the "Pauline" theology of the New Testament as presented in the Book of Romans.

Romans 5 (King James Version)

1Therefore being justified by faith, we have peace with God through our Lord Jesus Christ:

2By whom also we have access by faith into this grace wherein we stand, and rejoice in hope of the glory of God.

3And not only so, but we glory in tribulations also: knowing that tribulation worketh patience;

4And patience, experience; and experience, hope:

5And hope maketh not ashamed; because the love of God is shed abroad in our hearts by the Holy Ghost which is given unto us.

6For when we were yet without strength, in due time Christ died for the unGodly.

7For scarcely for a righteous man will one die: yet peradventure for a good man some would even dare to die.

8But God commendeth his love toward us, in that, while we were yet sinners, Christ died for us.

9Much more then, being now justified by his blood, we shall be saved from wrath through him.

10For if, when we were enemies, we were reconciled to God by the death of his Son, much more, being reconciled, we shall be saved by his life.

11And not only so, but we also joy in God through our Lord Jesus Christ, by whom we have now received the atonement.

12Wherefore, as by one man sin entered into the world, and death by sin; and so death passed upon all men, for that all have sinned:

13(For until the law sin was in the world: but sin is not imputed when there is no law.

14Nevertheless death reigned from Adam to Moses, even over them that had not sinned after the similitude of Adam's transgression, who is the figure of him that was to come.

15But not as the offence, so also is the free gift. For if through the offence of one many be dead, much more the grace of God, and the gift by grace, which is by one man, Jesus Christ, hath abounded unto many.

16And not as it was by one that sinned, so is the gift: for the judgment was by one to condemnation, but the free gift is of many offences unto justification.

17For if by one man's offence death reigned by one; much more they which receive abundance of grace and of the gift of righteousness shall reign in life by one, Jesus Christ.)

18Therefore as by the offence of one judgment came upon all men to condemnation; even so by the righteousness of one the free gift came upon all men unto justification of life.

19For as by one man's disobedience many were made sinners, so by the obedience of one shall many be made righteous.

20Moreover the law entered, that the offence might abound. But where sin abounded, grace did much more abound:

21That as sin hath reigned unto death, even so might grace reign through righteousness unto eternal life by Jesus Christ our Lord.

28) Then He continued; "You become sick and die because you did not have access to the knowledge of Him who can heal you.

29) If you have any sense, you must understand this.

This conversation reflects man's eternal attempt to make sense and give reason to why the world is such a cruel and arbitrary place. The ongoing questions of: "Why do bad things happen to good people?" or "What did I do to deserve this?" continues to haunt us as we seek the intelligence behind creation and existence.

In certain sects of Gnostic cosmology, the reason, or blame, for such irrational global malaise is placed on the Creator God. Because our knowledge of first century Gnostic cosmology is lacking, there is confusion as to exact beliefs of some sects when it comes to the Creator God.

According to John Lash in his essay of Gnosticism, February 2001:

"The emphasis on deviant forces called Archons is unique to Gnostic vision. Deviance runs deep into the cosmic pattern, but it operates through error rather than sin. The Christian notion of sin due to the Fall has no role in Gnostic theology. Gnostic teachings on "the generation of error" are among the most subtle and complex of any religious system. "The world came about through a mistake," says The Gospel of Philip (NHL II, 3). The world meant here is specifically our world-system, the solar system, not the entire cosmos. Gnostic cosmology seems to have been rigorous in ascribing the living, intelligent aspect of our world-system to the Aeons, while ascribing its mechanical or inorganic aspect to the Archons. Scholars wrongly perpetuate the notion that Gnosticism assumed two Supreme Gods, one good and the other evil, and rejected the visible world as the handiwork of the latter. Rather, it assumes two distinct world-orders emanated from the same source and then, somehow, collapsed into each other. The imperative of spiritual development is liberation from the deviant forces, not escape from the material world."

The assumption that most other scholars are mistaken in their understanding of Gnosticism is probably misplaced. More reasonable is the fact that various sects of Gnosticism had similar theology but somewhat divergent myths and cosmologies.

Some Gnostic sects seemed to believe that the creator of this physical world was a flawed and spiteful entity that imprisoned the human soul.

In the National Geographic Magazine, 2006, Karen Lang wrote:

"Gnostics saw the Old Testament God as a lower deity, a power crazed Demiurge, who created a flawed physical world that imprisons human souls. Salvation for them meant escaping the physical realm to be reunited with the true Supreme Being. To Gnostics, any defiance against the false Creator God was a heroic act. So one school of Gnostics celebrated Cain's murder of Abel, whose offering of lambs the Old Testament God favored over Cain's offering of crops. In the same way, the same school celebrated the people of Sodom, the city that the Old

Testament God destroys after its people try to rape visiting angels. These Gnostics were not embracing murder or rape, they were identifying with those who rebelled against the Old Testament God."

The discussion between Jesus and his disciples was one in which they were asking for explanation and clarification of the origin of suffering in the world.

30) The material world produced a great passion (desire or suffering) without equal. This was contrary to the natural balance. The entire cosmos (body of creation) was disturbed by it.

The passion referred to in the above verse may have been Sophia's passion to know the true God, the result of which brought about the perturbation of creation.

In the May, 2005 article on the site, Alternative Religions, Jennifer Emick reports:

" In Gnostic cosmology, Sophia (Holy Wisdom, or the Holy spirit), a divine emanation, seeks to know God, and in doing (so), falls outside the "Pleroma," the unified divine light. As She falls, she gives birth to the "blind Demiurge" Yaldabaoth, who is also Satan/Yahweh.

Yaldabaoth, who believes himself to be God, creates the material world and mankind, trapping Sophia within."

The passion could also be the ripple effect of Sophia's divine disturbance reflected in the sinful disposition of man as explained in the Book of Romans.

Romans 1 (King James Version)
22Professing themselves to be wise, they became fools,

23And changed the glory of the uncorruptible God into an image made like to corruptible man, and to birds, and four-footed beasts, and creeping things.

24Wherefore God also gave them up to uncleanness through the lusts of their own hearts, to dishonour their own bodies between themselves:

25Who changed the truth of God into a lie, and worshipped and served the creature more than the Creator, who is blessed for ever. Amen.

26For this cause God gave them up unto vile affections: for even their women did change the natural use into that which is against nature:

27And likewise also the men, leaving the natural use of the woman, burned in their lust one toward another; men with men working that which is unseemly, and receiving in themselves that recompence of their error which was meet.

28And even as they did not like to retain God in their knowledge, God gave them over to a reprobate mind, to do those things which are not convenient;

29Being filled with all unrighteousness, fornication, wickedness, covetousness, maliciousness; full of envy, murder, debate, deceit, malignity; whisperers,

30Backbiters, haters of God, despiteful, proud, boasters, inventors of evil things, disobedient to parents,

31Without understanding, covenant breakers, without natural affection, implacable, unmerciful:

32Who knowing the judgment of God, that they which commit such things are worthy of death, not only do the same, but have pleasure in them that do them.

Passion, in its basic form, is suffering. In most Eastern philosophies, disassociating oneself with the world can eliminate suffering. If there is no desire there is no suffering.

According to Lewis Loflin in his work, *Overview of Gnosticism*, "Gnosticism is loaded with Buddhism and other Eastern religions and also takes a negative view of the world and searches for "inner truth." There is also a great deal of neo-Platonism in both Gnosticism and Christianity in general."

Quoting Will Durant in *The Age of Faith*;

"In regards to Nicaea and the 4th century, neo-Platonism was still a power in religion and philosophy. Those doctrines which Plotinus had given a shadowy form of a triune spirit binding all reality, of a Logos or intermediary deity who had done the work of creation, of soul as divine and matter as flesh and evil, of spheres of existence along whose invisible stairs the soul had fallen from God to man and might extend from man to God these mystic ideas left their mark on the apostles John and Paul..." (P 9)

Loflin goes on to say, "Paul was a cultural Greek and John was a Greek convert. They wrote in Greek for a Greek audience. The Book of John and Revelation are Gnostic/Essene in origin. Paul was very revered by them but I wouldn't call Paul an outright Gnostic. His spiritual experience on the road to Damascus in Acts is typical Gnosticism or spiritual enlightenment."

31) That is why I said to you, Be encouraged, and if you are discouraged be encouraged when you see the different forms nature has taken.

The Psalmist, David, refers to the manifold works, or creations of God. The word, "manifold", means various, different, multicolored, or variegated.

Psalm 104 (King James Version)

1Bless the LORD, O my soul. O LORD my God, thou art very great; thou art clothed with honour and majesty.

2Who coverest thyself with light as with a garment: who stretchest out the heavens like a curtain:

3Who layeth the beams of his chambers in the waters: who maketh the clouds his chariot: who walketh upon the wings of the wind:

4Who maketh his angels spirits; his ministers a flaming fire:

5Who laid the foundations of the earth, that it should not be removed for ever.

6Thou coveredst it with the deep as with a garment: the waters stood above the mountains.

7At thy rebuke they fled; at the voice of thy thunder they hasted away.

8They go up by the mountains; they go down by the valleys unto the place which thou hast founded for them.

9Thou hast set a bound that they may not pass over; that they turn not again to cover the earth.

10He sendeth the springs into the valleys, which run among the hills.

11They give drink to every beast of the field: the wild asses quench their thirst.

12By them shall the fowls of the heaven have their habitation, which sing among the branches.

13He watereth the hills from his chambers: the earth is satisfied with the fruit of thy works.

14He causeth the grass to grow for the cattle, and herb for the service of man: that he may bring forth food out of the earth;

15And wine that maketh glad the heart of man, and oil to make his face to shine, and bread which strengtheneth man's heart.

16The trees of the LORD are full of sap; the cedars of Lebanon, which he hath planted;

17Where the birds make their nests: as for the stork, the fir trees are her house.

18The high hills are a refuge for the wild goats; and the rocks for the conies.

19He appointed the moon for seasons: the sun knoweth his going down.

20Thou makest darkness, and it is night: wherein all the beasts of the forest do creep forth.

21The young lions roar after their prey, and seek their meat from God.

22The sun ariseth, they gather themselves together, and lay them down in their dens.

23Man goeth forth unto his work and to his labour until the evening.

24O LORD, how manifold are thy works! in wisdom hast thou made them all: the earth is full of thy riches.

25So is this great and wide sea, wherein are things creeping innumerable, both small and great beasts.

26There go the ships: there is that leviathan, whom thou hast made to play therein.

27These wait all upon thee; that thou mayest give them their meat in due season.

28That thou givest them they gather: thou openest thine hand, they are filled with good.

29Thou hidest thy face, they are troubled: thou takest away their breath, they die, and return to their dust.

30Thou sendest forth thy spirit, they are created: and thou renewest the face of the earth.

32) He who has ears to hear, let him hear."

33) When the Blessed One had said this, He greeted all of them and said; "Peace be with you. Take my peace into you.

John 14:26-28 (King James Version)

26But the Comforter, which is the Holy Ghost, whom the Father will send in my name, he shall teach you all things, and bring all things to your remembrance, whatsoever I have said unto you.

27Peace I leave with you, my peace I give unto you: not as the world giveth, give I unto you. Let not your heart be troubled, neither let it be afraid.

28Ye have heard how I said unto you, I go away, and come again unto you. If ye loved me, ye would rejoice, because I said, I go unto the Father: for my Father is greater than I.

34) Beware that no one deceives you by saying, 'Look (he is) here or look (he is) there. The Son of Man is within you.'

35) Follow Him there.

36) Those who seek Him will find Him.

Luke 17:20-24 King James Version

20And when he was demanded of the Pharisees, when the kingdom of God should come, he answered them and said, The kingdom of God cometh not with observation:

21Neither shall they say, Lo here! or, lo there! for, behold, the kingdom of God is within you.

22And he said unto the disciples, The days will come, when ye shall desire to see one of the days of the Son of man, and ye shall not see it.

23And they shall say to you, See here; or, see there: go not after them, nor follow them.

24For as the lightning, that lighteneth out of the one part under heaven, shineth unto the other part under heaven; so shall also the Son of man be in his day.

Matthew 24:23-30 (King James Version)

23Then if any man shall say unto you, Lo, here is Christ, or there; believe it not.

24For there shall arise false Christs, and false prophets, and shall shew great signs and wonders; insomuch that, if it were possible, they shall deceive the very elect.

25Behold, I have told you before.

26Wherefore if they shall say unto you, Behold, he is in the desert; go not forth: behold, he is in the secret chambers; believe it not.

27For as the lightning cometh out of the east, and shineth even unto the west; so shall also the coming of the Son of man be.

28For wheresoever the carcase is, there will the eagles be gathered together.

29Immediately after the tribulation of those days shall the sun be darkened, and the moon shall not give her light, and the stars shall fall from heaven, and the powers of the heavens shall be shaken:

30And then shall appear the sign of the Son of man in heaven: and then shall all the tribes of the earth mourn, and they shall see the Son of man coming in the clouds of heaven with power and great glory.

37) Go now and preach the gospel (this good news) of the Kingdom.

Mark 16:14-16 (King James Version)
14Afterward he appeared unto the eleven as they sat at meat, and upbraided them with their unbelief and hardness of heart, because they believed not them which had seen him after he was risen.
15And he said unto them, Go ye into all the world, and preach the gospel to every creature.
16He that believeth and is baptized shall be saved; but he that believeth not shall be damned.

38) Do not lay down any rules other than what I told you, and do not give a law like the lawgivers (Pharisees) or you will be held to account for the same laws."

Matthew 11:29-31 (King James Version)
29Take my yoke upon you, and learn of me; for I am meek and lowly in heart: and ye shall find rest unto your souls.
30For my yoke is easy, and my burden is light.

Luke 11:46-50 (King James Version)

46And he said, Woe unto you also, ye lawyers! for ye lade men with burdens grievous to be borne, and ye yourselves touch not the burdens with one of your fingers.

47Woe unto you! for ye build the sepulchres of the prophets, and your fathers killed them.

48Truly ye bear witness that ye allow the deeds of your fathers: for they indeed killed them, and ye build their sepulchres.

49Therefore also said the wisdom of God, I will send them prophets and apostles, and some of them they shall slay and persecute:

50That the blood of all the prophets, which was shed from the foundation of the world, may be required of this generation;

39) When He said this He departed.

Chapter 5

1) Then they were troubled and wept out loud, saying, "How shall we go to the Gentiles and preach the gospel of the Kingdom of the Son of Man? If they did not spare Him, how can we expect that they will spare us?"

2) Then Mary stood up, greeted them all, and said to her fellow believers, "Do not weep and do not be troubled and do not waver, because His grace will be with you completely and it will protect you.

The prominence of women in the early church is well documented. The same Greek word used for deacon is also used when referring to women serving the church.

Romans 16 (King James Version)
1I commend unto you Phebe our sister, which is a servant of the church which is at Cenchrea:
2That ye receive her in the Lord, as becometh saints, and that ye assist her in whatsoever business she hath need of you: for she hath been a succourer of many, and of myself also.
3Greet Priscilla and Aquila my helpers in Christ Jesus:
4Who have for my life laid down their own necks: unto whom not only I give thanks, but also all the churches of the Gentiles.

As to their fear, the following scriptures apply.

Romans 8:9-25 (King James Version)
9But ye are not in the flesh, but in the Spirit, if so be that the Spirit of God dwell in you. Now if any man have not the Spirit of Christ, he is

none of his.

10And if Christ be in you, the body is dead because of sin; but the Spirit is life because of righteousness.

11But if the Spirit of him that raised up Jesus from the dead dwell in you, he that raised up Christ from the dead shall also quicken your mortal bodies by his Spirit that dwelleth in you.

12Therefore, brethren, we are debtors, not to the flesh, to live after the flesh.

13For if ye live after the flesh, ye shall die: but if ye through the Spirit do mortify the deeds of the body, ye shall live.

14For as many as are led by the Spirit of God, they are the sons of God.

15For ye have not received the spirit of bondage again to fear; but ye have received the Spirit of adoption, whereby we cry, Abba, Father.

16The Spirit itself beareth witness with our spirit, that we are the children of God:

17And if children, then heirs; heirs of God, and joint-heirs with Christ; if so be that we suffer with him, that we may be also glorified together.

18For I reckon that the sufferings of this present time are not worthy to be compared with the glory which shall be revealed in us.

19For the earnest expectation of the creature waiteth for the manifestation of the sons of God.

20For the creature was made subject to vanity, not willingly, but by reason of him who hath subjected the same in hope,

21Because the creature itself also shall be delivered from the bondage of corruption into the glorious liberty of the children of God.

22For we know that the whole creation groaneth and travaileth in pain together until now.

23And not only they, but ourselves also, which have the firstfruits of the Spirit, even we ourselves groan within ourselves, waiting for the adoption, to wit, the redemption of our body.

24For we are saved by hope: but hope that is seen is not hope: for what a man seeth, why doth he yet hope for?

25But if we hope for that we see not, then do we with patience wait for it.

3) Instead, let us praise His greatness, because He has prepared us and made us into mature (finished or complete) people."

4) Mary's words turned their hearts to the Good, and they began to discuss the words of the Savior.

Romans 8:35-39 (King James Version)
35Who shall separate us from the love of Christ? shall tribulation, or distress, or persecution, or famine, or nakedness, or peril, or sword?

36As it is written, For thy sake we are killed all the day long; we are accounted as sheep for the slaughter.

37Nay, in all these things we are more than conquerors through him that loved us.

38For I am persuaded, that neither death, nor life, nor angels, nor principalities, nor powers, nor things present, nor things to come,

39Nor height, nor depth, nor any other creature, shall be able to separate us from the love of God, which is in Christ Jesus our Lord.

5) Peter said to Mary, "Sister we know that the Savior loved you more than all other women.

The expression and mode of this love is not defined or explained, only that it was obvious to all.

6) Tell us the words of the Savior that you remember and know, but we have not heard and do not know."

7) Mary answered him and said, "I will tell you what He hid from you."

Luke 8 (King James Version)

16No man, when he hath lighted a candle, covereth it with a vessel, or putteth it under a bed; but setteth it on a candlestick, that they which enter in may see the light.

17For nothing is secret, that shall not be made manifest; neither any thing hid, that shall not be known and come abroad.

18Take heed therefore how ye hear: for whosoever hath, to him shall be given; and whosoever hath not, from him shall be taken even that which he seemeth to have.

8) And she began to speak these words to them: She said, "I saw the Lord in a vision and I said to Him, 'Lord I saw you today in a vision.'

9) He answered and said to me; 'You will be happy that you did not waver at the sight of Me. Where the mind is there is the treasure.'

Matthew 6 (King James Version)

19Lay not up for yourselves treasures upon earth, where moth and rust doth corrupt, and where thieves break through and steal:

20But lay up for yourselves treasures in heaven, where neither moth nor rust doth corrupt, and where thieves do not break through nor steal:

21For where your treasure is, there will your heart be also.

22The light of the body is the eye: if therefore thine eye be single, thy whole body shall be full of light.

23But if thine eye be evil, thy whole body shall be full of darkness. If therefore the light that is in thee be darkness, how great is that darkness!

10) I said to Him; 'Lord, does one see visions through the soul or through the spirit?'

According to Watchman Nee, man is a three-fold entity. The complete person is a body, soul, and spirit.

His soul is the will and mind, which has the power of the breath of God in it from that time when God breathed into man and he became a living soul. It is this part of man that gives him the power to manipulate time, space, and the outcome of things. It is his lost "God power." The will and mind can be focused and the result is a manipulation of things according to the will of man. However, the soul is selfish, prideful, and deceitful. As man takes control, things fall apart.

In his answer, Jesus draws yet another line of distinction between the mind and will. This division leaves the soul defined as the will of a person. The mind is left outside the structure and becomes the point of contact between the will of man and the spirit, which is connected to God. Its function would be to mediate, decide, and control which direction man proceeds.

The spirit is that direct connection to God. It is given by him and returns to him. It cannot be destroyed. It is the essence of what we are. Assuming we are the same person in our deepest core even after a stroke or accident, it must not be the mind or soul that defines us, but the spirit that is who and what we are.

11) The Savior answered and said; 'He sees visions through neither the soul nor the spirit. It is through the mind that is between the two. That is what sees the vision and it is (there the vision exists).'"

(Pages 11 - 14 are missing. Text begins again at chapter 8)

Chapter 8

10) And Desire, (a lesser God, Archon), said, "Before, I did not see you descending, but now I see you ascending. Why do you lie since you belong to me?"

These "lesser Gods" are part of the mythos of Gnosticism. Sophia created the lesser God who created the material world. Along with creation of this God, called the Demiurge, or half-maker, the Archons were created. These are Gods who are below his station, equivalent to angels. Desire, Ignorance and others are part of the company of these Archons.

According the research done by the Christian Apologetic Research Ministry,

"The unknowable God was far too pure and perfect to have anything to do with the material universe which was considered evil. Therefore, God generated lesser divinities, or emanations. One of these emanations, Wisdom desired to know the unknowable God. Out of this erring desire the Demiurge an evil God was formed and it was this evil God that created the universe. He along with Archons kept the mortals in bondage in material matter and tried to prevent the pure spirit souls from ascending back to God after the death of the physical bodies.

Since, according to the Gnostics, matter is evil, deliverance from material form was attainable only through special knowledge revealed by special Gnostic teachers. Christ was the divine redeemer who descended from the spiritual realm to reveal the knowledge necessary for this redemption. In conclusion, Gnosticism is dualistic. That is, it teaches there is a good and evil, spirit and matter, light and dark, etc. dualism in the universe."

Ephesians 6:12 (King James Version)
12For we wrestle not against flesh and blood, but against principalities, against powers, against the rulers of the darkness of this world, against spiritual wickedness in high places.

Note that in the Greek version the direct connection is established between our trials and the Archons. The transliteration is added beside the Greek word.

Ephesians 6:12 1550 Stephanus New Testament (Greek Version) -
Because it is not up to us to wrestle against blood and flesh, but against the (ARCHAS) rulers, against the authorities, against the world's rulers of darkness of this age, against the spiritual powers in the heavenlies.

11) The soul answered and said, "I saw you but you did not see me nor recognize me. I covered you like a garment and you did not know me."

12) When it said this, the soul went away greatly rejoicing.

13) Again it came to the third power (lesser God, Archon), which is called Ignorance.

Ephesians 4 (New International Version)

17So I tell you this, and insist on it in the Lord, that you must no longer live as the Gentiles do, in the futility of their thinking. 18They are darkened in their understanding and separated from the life of God because of the ignorance that is in them due to the hardening of their hearts. 19Having lost all sensitivity, they have given themselves over to sensuality so as to indulge in every kind of impurity, with a continual lust for more.

20You, however, did not come to know Christ that way. 21Surely you heard of him and were taught in him in accordance with the truth that is in Jesus. 22You were taught, with regard to your former way of life, to put off your old self, which is being corrupted by its deceitful desires; 23to be made new in the attitude of your minds; 24and to put on the new self, created to be like God in true righteousness and holiness.

14) The power questioned the soul, saying, "Where are you going? You are enslaved (captured) in wickedness. Since you are its captive you cannot judge (have no judgment)."

2 Timothy 3 (King James Version)

1This know also, that in the last days perilous times shall come.

2For men shall be lovers of their own selves, covetous, boasters, proud, blasphemers, disobedient to parents, unthankful, unholy,

3Without natural affection, trucebreakers, false accusers, incontinent, fierce, despisers of those that are good,

4Traitors, heady, highminded, lovers of pleasures more than lovers of God;

5Having a form of Godliness, but denying the power thereof: from such turn away.

6For of this sort are they which creep into houses, and lead captive silly women laden with sins, led away with divers lusts,

7Ever learning, and never able to come to the knowledge of the truth.

15) And the soul said, "Why do you judge me, when I have not judged?"

16) "I was captured, although I have not captured anyone."

17) "I was not recognized. But I have recognized that God (the All) is in (has been dissolved into / is a part of) both the earthly things and in the heavenly (things)."

This seems somewhat contradictory to staunch Gnostic theology, which views the material world as opposed to God, having been created and held hostage by Aeons, Archons, and a ruthless Demiurge. According to this view, God, who is holy, can have nothing to do with the material world, which is full of sin or error. Gnostics tend to view the problems in the world as a product of error and not sin.

It is difficult to reconcile Gnosticism and pantheism since pantheists believe God is in and part of all things , thus all things are part of God, and Gnostics believe the holy and Supreme God can have nothing to do with the corrupt material world.

Ephesians 4:5-6 (King James Version)
5One Lord, one faith, one baptism,
6One God and Father of all, who is above all, and through all, and in you all.

18) When the soul had overcome the third power, it ascended and saw the fourth power, which took seven forms.

19) The first form is darkness, the second desire, the third ignorance, the fourth is the lust of death, the fifth is the dominion of the flesh, the sixth is the empty useless wisdom of flesh, the seventh is the wisdom of vengeance and anger. These are the seven powers of wrath.

The list of darkness, desire, lust, fleshly drives, worldly wisdom, anger, wrath, and vengeance fall into two categories. Darkness, ignorance, and worldly wisdom address the lack of knowledge or gnosis that would set one free from the material world. Lust, desires, vengeance, anger, and wrath speak to the captivity of mind and emotion that keeps us distracted from the truth or our lack of the divine knowledge.

Ephesians 2 (King James Version)
1And you hath he quickened, who were dead in trespasses and sins;
2Wherein in time past ye walked according to the course of this world, according to the prince of the power of the air, the spirit that now worketh in the children of disobedience:
3Among whom also we all had our conversation in times past in the lusts of our flesh, fulfilling the desires of the flesh and of the mind; and were by nature the children of wrath, even as others.
4But God, who is rich in mercy, for his great love wherewith he loved us,

5Even when we were dead in sins, hath quickened us together with Christ, (by grace ye are saved;)

6And hath raised us up together, and made us sit together in heavenly places in Christ Jesus:

7That in the ages to come he might shew the exceeding riches of his grace in his kindness toward us through Christ Jesus.

8For by grace are ye saved through faith; and that not of yourselves: it is the gift of God:

9Not of works, lest any man should boast.

10For we are his workmanship, created in Christ Jesus unto good works, which God hath before ordained that we should walk in them.

11Wherefore remember, that ye being in time past Gentiles in the flesh, who are called Uncircumcision by that which is called the Circumcision in the flesh made by hands;

12That at that time ye were without Christ, being aliens from the commonwealth of Israel, and strangers from the covenants of promise, having no hope, and without God in the world:

13But now in Christ Jesus ye who sometimes were far off are made nigh by the blood of Christ.

14For he is our peace, who hath made both one, and hath broken down the middle wall of partition between us;

15Having abolished in his flesh the enmity, even the law of commandments contained in ordinances; for to make in himself of twain one new man, so making peace;

16And that he might reconcile both unto God in one body by the cross, having slain the enmity thereby:

17And came and preached peace to you which were afar off, and to them that were nigh.

18For through him we both have access by one Spirit unto the Father.

1 John 2 (King James Version)

9He that saith he is in the light, and hateth his brother, is in darkness even until now.

10He that loveth his brother abideth in the light, and there is none occasion of stumbling in him.

11But he that hateth his brother is in darkness, and walketh in darkness, and knoweth not whither he goeth, because that darkness hath blinded his eyes.

12I write unto you, little children, because your sins are forgiven you for his name's sake.

13I write unto you, fathers, because ye have known him that is from the beginning. I write unto you, young men, because ye have overcome the wicked one. I write unto you, little children, because ye have known the Father.

14I have written unto you, fathers, because ye have known him that is from the beginning. I have written unto you, young men, because ye are strong, and the word of God abideth in you, and ye have overcome the wicked one.

15Love not the world, neither the things that are in the world. If any man love the world, the love of the Father is not in him.

16For all that is in the world, the lust of the flesh, and the lust of the eyes, and the pride of life, is not of the Father, but is of the world.

17And the world passeth away, and the lust thereof: but he that doeth the will of God abideth for ever.

20) They asked the soul, "Where do you come from, slayer of men: where are you going, conqueror of space?"

The soul is our errant will and emotions. They give rise to lust, desire, and anger, which keep us ignorant and blind us from the gnosis.

21) The soul answered and said, "What has trapped me has been slain, and what kept me caged has been overcome."

22) "My desire has been ended, and ignorance has died."

23) "In an age (dispensation) I was released from the world in a symbolic image, and I was released from the chains of oblivion, which were only temporary (in this transient world)."

In our own time, according to the will of God, we are brought into the knowledge of the truth. Nothing changes, but our souls are released. As it is written by Lao Tsu, "Before enlightenment, carrying water and chopping wood. After enlightenment, carrying water and chopping wood." Any change is symbolic of the internal gnosis.

24) "From this time on I will attain the rest of the ages and seasons of silence."

Matthew 11:28 (King James Version)

28Come unto me, all ye that labour and are heavy laden, and I will give you rest.

Chapter 9

1) When Mary had said this, she fell silent, since she had shared all the Savior had told her.

2) But Andrew said to the other believers, "Say what you want about what she has said, but I do not believe that the Savior said this. These teachings are very strange ideas."

Traditional Judaism has no parallel or similar belief. Some may see traditional Christianity as the fulfillment of Jewish theology but certain parts of Gnostic theology has no such foundation.

Some scholars believe that Gnostic roots can be traced to the older wisdom religions of Egypt. Both Christians and Jews reject the wisdom religions.

3) Peter answered him and spoke concerning these things.

4) He questioned them about the Savior and asked, "Did He really speak privately with a woman and not openly to us? Are we to turn around and all listen to her? Did He prefer her to us?"

The following two verses show the difference in how traditional Christianity treats women as opposed to how Jesus treated women.

1 Corinthians 14:34 (King James Version)

34Let your women keep silence in the churches: for it is not permitted unto them to speak; but they are commanded to be under obedience as also saith the law.

John 8 (King James Version)

1Jesus went unto the mount of Olives.

2And early in the morning he came again into the temple, and all the people came unto him; and he sat down, and taught them.

3And the scribes and Pharisees brought unto him a woman taken in adultery; and when they had set her in the midst,

4They say unto him, Master, this woman was taken in adultery, in the very act.

5Now Moses in the law commanded us, that such should be stoned: but what sayest thou?

6This they said, tempting him, that they might have to accuse him. But Jesus stooped down, and with his finger wrote on the ground, as though he heard them not.

7So when they continued asking him, he lifted up himself, and said unto them, He that is without sin among you, let him first cast a stone at her.

8And again he stooped down, and wrote on the ground.

9And they which heard it, being convicted by their own conscience, went out one by one, beginning at the eldest, even unto the last: and

Jesus was left alone, and the woman standing in the midst.

10When Jesus had lifted up himself, and saw none but the woman, he said unto her, Woman, where are those thine accusers? hath no man condemned thee?

11She said, No man, Lord. And Jesus said unto her, Neither do I condemn thee: go, and sin no more.

5) Then Mary sobbed and said to Peter, "My brother Peter, what do you think? Do you think that I have made all of this up in my heart by myself? Do you think that I am lying about the Savior?"

6) Levi said to Peter, "Peter you have always had a hot temper.

7) Now I see you fighting against this woman like she was your enemy."

8) If the Savior made her worthy, who are you to reject her? What do you think you are doing? Surely the Savior knows her well?

9) That is why He loved her more than us. Let us be ashamed of this and let us put on the perfect Man. Let us separate from

each other as He commanded us to do so we can preach the gospel, not laying down any other rule or other law beyond what the Savior told us."

10) And when they heard this they began to go out and proclaim and preach.

Romans 10 (King James Version)

1Brethren, my heart's desire and prayer to God for Israel is, that they might be saved.

2For I bear them record that they have a zeal of God, but not according to knowledge.

3For they being ignorant of God's righteousness, and going about to establish their own righteousness, have not submitted themselves unto the righteousness of God.

4For Christ is the end of the law for righteousness to every one that believeth.

5For Moses describeth the righteousness which is of the law, That the man which doeth those things shall live by them.

6But the righteousness which is of faith speaketh on this wise, Say not in thine heart, Who shall ascend into heaven? (that is, to bring Christ down from above:)

7Or, Who shall descend into the deep? (that is, to bring up Christ again from the dead.)

8But what saith it? The word is nigh thee, even in thy mouth, and in thy heart: that is, the word of faith, which we preach;

9That if thou shalt confess with thy mouth the Lord Jesus, and shalt believe in thine heart that God hath raised him from the dead, thou shalt be saved.

10For with the heart man believeth unto righteousness; and with the mouth confession is made unto salvation.

11For the scripture saith, Whosoever believeth on him shall not be ashamed.

12For there is no difference between the Jew and the Greek: for the same Lord over all is rich unto all that call upon him.

13For whosoever shall call upon the name of the Lord shall be saved.

14How then shall they call on him in whom they have not believed? and how shall they believe in him of whom they have not heard? and how shall they hear without a preacher?

15And how shall they preach, except they be sent? as it is written, How beautiful are the feet of them that preach the gospel of peace, and bring glad tidings of good things!

The Gospel of Mary Magdalene
(Text Only)

(Pages 1 to 6, containing chapters 1 to 3, could not be recovered. The text starts on page 7, chapter 4)

Chapter 4

21 (And they asked Jesus), "Will matter then be destroyed or not?"

22) The Savior said, "All nature, all things formed, and all creatures exist in and with one another, and they will be dissolved again into their own elements (origins).

23) This is because it is the nature of matter to return to its original elements.

24) If you have an ear to hear, listen to this."

25) Peter said to him, "Since you have explained all things to us, tell us this also: What sin did the world commit (what sin is in the world)?"

26) The Savior said, "There is no sin (of the world). Each person makes his own sin when he does things like adultery (in the same nature as adultery). This is called sin.

27) That is why the Good came to be among you. He came to restore every nature to its basic root."

28) Then He continued; "You become sick and die because you did not have access to (knowledge of) Him who can heal you.

29) If you have any sense, you must understand this.

30) The material world produced a great passion (desire or suffering) without equal. This was contrary to the natural balance. The entire cosmos (body) was disturbed by it.

31) That is why I said to you, Be encouraged, and if you are discouraged be encouraged when you see the different forms nature has taken.

32) He who has ears to hear, let him hear."

33) When the Blessed One had said this, He greeted all of them and said; "Peace be with you. Take my peace into you.

34) Beware that no one deceives you by saying, 'Look (he is) here or look (he is) there. The Son of Man is within you.'

35) Follow Him there.

36) Those who seek Him will find Him.

37) Go now and preach the gospel (this good news) of the Kingdom.

38) Do not lay down any rules beyond what I told you, and do not give a law like the lawgivers (Pharisees) or you will be held to account for the same laws."

39) When He said this He departed.

Chapter 5

1) Then they were troubled and wept out loud, saying, "How shall we go to the Gentiles and preach the gospel of the Kingdom of the Son of Man? If they did not spare Him, how can we expect that they will spare us?"

2) Then Mary stood up, greeted them all, and said to her fellow believers, "Do not weep and do not be troubled and do not waver, because His grace will be with you completely and it will protect you.

3) Instead, let us praise His greatness, because He has prepared us and made us into mature (finished or complete) people."

4) Mary's words turned their hearts to the Good, and they began to discuss the words of the Savior.

5) Peter said to Mary, "Sister we know that the Savior loved you more than all other women.

6) Tell us the words of the Savior that you remember and know, but we have not heard and do not know."

7) Mary answered him and said, "I will tell you what He hid from you."

8) And she began to speak these words to them: She said, "I saw the Lord in a vision and I said to Him, 'Lord I saw you today in a vision.'

9) He answered and said to me; 'You will be happy that you did not waver at the sight of Me. Where the mind is there is the treasure.'

10) I said to Him; 'Lord, does one see visions through the soul or through the spirit?'

11) The Savior answered and said; 'He sees visions through neither the soul nor the spirit. It is through the mind that is between the two. That is what sees the vision and it is (there the vision exists).'"

(Pages 11 to 14 are missing. Text begins again at chapter 8)

Chapter 8

10) And Desire, (a lesser God), said, "Before, I did not see you descending, but now I see you ascending. Why do you lie since you belong to me?"

11) The soul answered and said, "I saw you but you did not see me nor recognize me. I covered you like a garment and you did not know me."

12) When it said this, the soul went away greatly rejoicing.

13) Again it came to the third power (lesser God), which is called Ignorance.

14) The power questioned the soul, saying, "Where are you going? You are enslaved (captured) in wickedness. Since you are its captive you cannot judge (have no judgment)."

15) And the soul said, "Why do you judge me, when I have not judged?"

16) "I was captured, although I have not captured anyone."

17) "I was not recognized. But I have recognized that God (the All) is in (being dissolved), both the earthly things and in the heavenly (things)."

18) When the soul had overcome the third power, it ascended and saw the fourth power, which took seven forms.

19) The first form is darkness, the second desire, the third ignorance, the fourth is the lust of death, the fifth is the dominion of the flesh, the sixth is the empty useless wisdom of flesh, the seventh is the wisdom of vengeance and anger. These are the seven powers of wrath.

20) They asked the soul, "Where do you come from, slayer of men: where are you going, conqueror of space?"

21) The soul answered and said, "What has trapped me has been slain, and what kept me caged has been overcome."

22) "My desire has been ended, and ignorance has died."

23) "In an age (dispensation) I was released from the world in a symbolic image, and I was released from the chains of

oblivion, which were only temporary (in this transient world)."

24) "From this time on I will attain the rest of the ages and seasons of silence."

Chapter 9

1) When Mary had said this, she fell silent, since she had shared all the Savior had told her.

2) But Andrew said to the other believers, "Say what you want about what she has said, but I do not believe that the Savior said this. These teachings are very strange ideas."

3) Peter answered him and spoke concerning these things.

4) He questioned them about the Savior and asked, "Did He really speak privately with a woman and not openly to us? Are we to turn around and all listen to her? Did He prefer her to us?"

5) Then Mary sobbed and said to Peter, "My brother Peter, what do you think? Do you think that I have made all of this

up in my heart by myself? Do you think that I am lying about the Savior?"

6) Levi said to Peter, "Peter you have always had a hot temper.

7) Now I see you fighting against this woman like she was your enemy."

8) If the Savior made her worthy, who are you to reject her? What do you think you are doing? Surely the Savior knows her well?

9) That is why He loved her more than us. Let us be ashamed of this and let us put on the perfect Man. Let us separate from each other as He commanded us to do so we can preach the gospel, not laying down any other rule or other law beyond what the Savior told us."

10) And when they heard this they began to go out and proclaim and preach.

Joseph B. Lumpkin

ABOUT THE AUTHOR

Joseph Lumpkin has written for various newspapers and is the author of a number of books on the subjects of religion and philosophy including the best selling book, *The Lost Book Of Enoch: A Comprehensive Transliteration*, published by Fifth Estate Publishers.

Joseph holds his Doctorate in the field of Ministry. He lives near Birmingham, Alabama with his wife, Lynn, and his son, Breandan. He teaches, lectures, and writes as life allows.

Look for other fine books by Joseph Lumpkin.

The Lost Book Of Enoch: A Comprehensive Transliteration,
ISBN: 0974633666

The Gospel of Thomas: A Contemporary Translation
ISBN: 0976823349

Fallen Angels, The Watchers, and the Origins of Evil:
A Problem of Choice
ISBN: 1933580100

Dark Night of the Soul - A Journey to the Heart of God

Joseph B. Lumpkin

ISBN: 0974633631

The Tao Te Ching: A Contemporary Translation
ISBN: 0976823314

Christian Counseling – Healing the Tribes of Man
ISBN: 1933589970

The Gnostic Gospels of Philip, Mary Magdalene, and Thomas:
Inside The Da Vinci Code and Holy Blood, Holy Grail
ISBN: 1933580135

The Book of Jubilees; The Little Genesis, The Apocalypse of Moses
ISBN: 1933580097

THE BOOK OF JASHER
The J. H. Parry Text in Modern English
ISBN: 1933580143

THE LOST BOOKS OF THE OLD TESTAMENT
ISBN: 1933580119

Printed in the United States
123312LV00003B/2/A

9 781933 580241